BASIC
RHYTHMIC TRAINING

Robert Starer

Robert Starer, distinguished composer, taught at the Julliard School from 1949 to 1974. Since 1963 he has been Professor of Music at Brooklyn College and the Graduate Center of the City University of New York.

ISBN 978-0-88188-449-4

HAL•LEONARD®
CORPORATION
7777 W. BLUEMOUND RD. P.O. BOX 13819 MILWAUKEE, WI 53213

Visit Hal Leonard Online at
www.halleonard.com

FOREWORD

BASIC RHYTHMIC TRAINING deals only with rhythm. It can be used in conjunction with any system of melodic ear-training. It is intended for the general music class, the conservatory-type course in musicianship, the private studio and for self-training. It is suitable for the young and the adult beginner.

The book assumes no prior knowledge. It begins with elementary rhythmic notation and since it gets progressively more complex, students with previous training will find their place when they encounter their first difficulty.

The exercises in this book should be performed in different ways and those ways should be changed frequently. The top line can be sung, hummed or spoken on a neutral syllable. The pulse can be tapped with a finger on the table or desk, tapped with a foot, clapped or conducted.

At the end of each section students are asked to make up their own examples. This is an important aspect of rhythmic training and should not be slighted. The examples made up by students can be used as additional material for dictation.

When the student completes this book, he or she may continue with chapter five of my book RHYTHMIC TRAINING, which goes into more advanced musical material.

Robert Starer

CONTENTS

A. MUSICAL RHYTHM AND THE PULSE

I. Notes and Rests Lasting 1, 2, 3 and 4 Beats

Rhythm is everywhere around us.

Day and night follow each other in rhythm.

So do the seasons: spring, summer, fall and winter.

There is rhythm even within us: our heart-beat which makes the blood flow. To feel it, you must surround the wrist of your left hand with the thumb and first finger of the right (or the other way around) and press, quite hard. When you do it right, you will feel the pulse, your own pulse. It is very even and steady.

Musical rhythm also has a pulse. In this book the pulse is written on the bottom line:

Let us create our own steady, even pulse.

First by tapping one foot.

Now by clapping our hands.

Next by saying: do, do, do, do, or ta, ta, ta, ta, or any other syllable you like.

Now by singing: la, la, la, la, on any note you like.

When we are excited, our pulse goes a little faster; when we are drowsy or bored, it goes a little slower. In music the speed of the pulse is called *tempo*.

When we walk, we produce a very even pulse. Also when we breathe. But it does not have to be like that. Let us inhale slowly and let the air out quickly. Let us inhale air for four beats of the pulse and then let it out for two beats:

In music it would look like this:

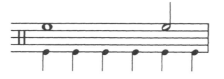

o   means four beats of the pulse.

   stands for two beats of the pulse.

(The stem makes the difference.)

Let us do it a few times.

Now let us do it the other way round: inhale for two beats and let the air out for four. It would look like this in music:

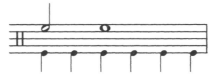

Now let us tap the beat with our foot and sing *la* on every other beat. In music it would look like this:

Let us do the same thing by clapping our hands on every beat and saying *do* on every other beat.

The musical sign that lasts for three beats looks like this: it has a stem and a little dot next to it. ♩.

Let us try it:

We already know the symbol for holding the sound we make for four beats. Let us do it either by singing or by speaking:

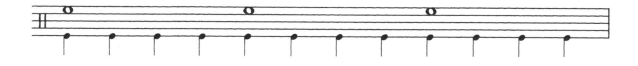

A long time ago music must have been sung more slowly than it is now. Therefore ○ is called a whole note, ♩ is called a half-note and the sign we have been using for the pulse ♩ is called a quarter-note. The one that lasts for three beats is called a dotted half: ♩.

Let us try the next three examples by singing or speaking the upper line and tapping or clapping the pulse:

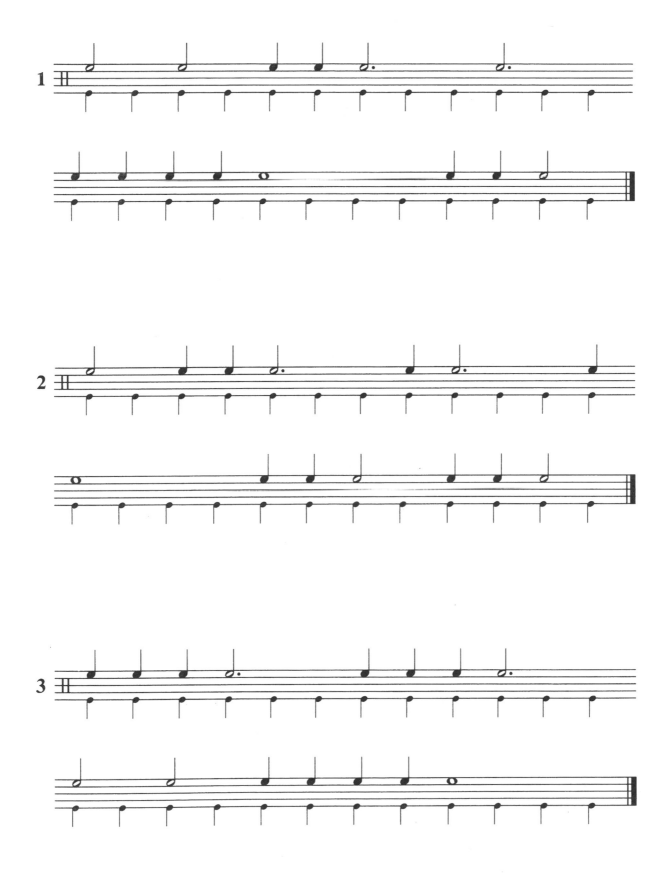

In music silence is also measured.

The sign for being silent for a single beat of the pulse is:

The sign for not making a sound for two beats is:

The rest, as we call the sign that tells us to be silent for two beats, sits on the third line.

The rest for three beats is the same with a dot next to it.

The rest for four beats hangs under the fourth line:

Let us practice rests:

Be sure you are absolutely silent when there is a rest. Otherwise

would sound the same as  It must not.

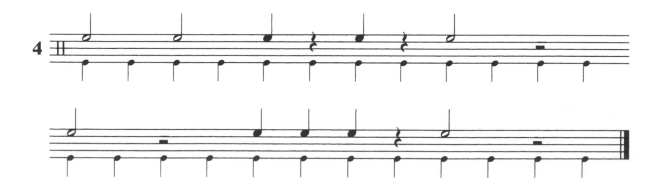

II. Downbeat and Upbeat; $\frac{2}{4}$ Time; The Tie

When you walk, each time you have used both feet, one after another, you have taken a full step. In music we call such a unit a *bar* or a *measure*. Bars are indicated by a line. If there are two quarter-note beats for each bar, we call it $\frac{2}{4}$ time:

When you use a hammer to drive in a nail, you are either hitting the nail or raising your arm to hit it again. Hitting the nail would be a strong beat (a downbeat); raising your arm would be a weak beat (an upbeat).

In $\frac{2}{4}$ time the first beat is always the downbeat, the second is the upbeat. In our book we shall show strong beats lower than weak beats on the staff. Like this:

Strong,   Weak,   etc.

Did you make the downbeat different from the upbeat in your tapping or clapping? Be sure that you do.

If you were to conduct rather than tap or clap, your arms should move like this:

When a note is connected to another note by a tie
across the bar line

the note at the end of the tie is not sounded. It is added to the note at the beginning
of the tie.

This can happen over several bars:

A piece of music can begin on an upbeat rather than on a downbeat. When that happens, a beat is taken off the last measure to make up for the one lost in the first.

When there is sound on the upbeat but none on the downbeat for more than one bar, it is called syncopation. There is much syncopation in jazz but also in many other kinds of music.

You will find syncopated rhythms with use of ties:

It can also be done with rests:

Make up two examples of your own using ties and rests. Be sure you have exactly two beats of pulse in each measure.

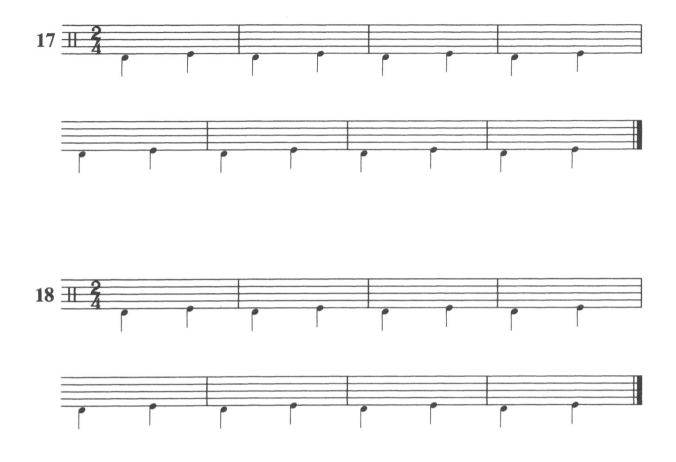

III. $\frac{3}{4}$ Time; Beginning on an Upbeat; Syncopation

In nature and all around us the rhythm of two, or duple meter, is the rhythm most widely found: up and down, in an out, day and night.

Human beings have been equally fond of three-time, or triple meter, as it is called. Many years ago people called 2-time the walking meter and 3-time the dancing meter. It is quite natural to hop or dance in three-time.

14

In $\frac{3}{4}$ time the first beat is strong, it is again the downbeat; the second and third beats are both weak:

Let us just tap the pulse. Be sure the first beat is stronger than the other two.

Now let us conduct. Your arms should move like this:

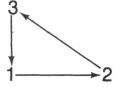

Here are some rhythms in triple time:

There are rests in triple time:

There are also ties in triple time:

In triple meter two types of upbeat are possible.
An upbeat of a single note:

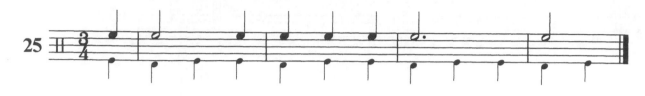

(notice that the last bar has only 2 beats)

Or an upbeat of two notes:

(notice that the last bar has only 1 beat)

Make up two examples of your own, using ties and rests. Be sure that each measure has exactly three beats, no more and no less.

IV. $\frac{4}{4}$ Time; Different Upbeats; More Syncopation

In music four-time is not the same as two times two. There is a difference between the first and the third beat; the third is a little weaker. But it is still stronger than the second and fourth beat; they are both weak.

Like this:

strong   weak   medium strong   weak

Let us tap the pulse. You need to make three different kinds of sound now:

If you conduct, the motion of your arms should look like this:

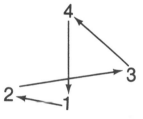

Here are some rhythms in four-time:

There are ties and rests in four-time:

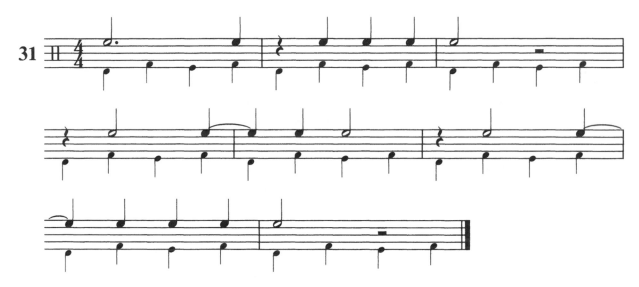

Yes, there is also syncopation.

In four-time three types of upbeat are possible.

An upbeat of a single note:

33

(the last bar has only 3 beats)

Or an upbeat of two notes:

34

(the last bar has only 2 beats)

Or an upbeat of three notes:

35

(the last bar has only one beat)

Make up two examples of your own in four-time. Do use rests and ties:

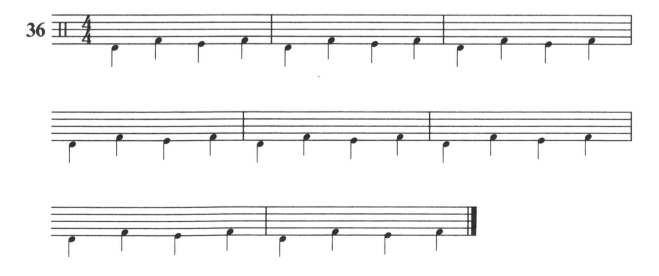

36

V. $\frac{5}{4}$ Time and Changing Meters

Before our century most music was in two, three, or four-time. There was also six, nine, and twelve-time, and we shall get to them later. Now we want to look into five-time and changing meters, which are becoming very popular these days.

Let us look into five-time first. It is either $2 + 3$ or $3 + 2$

The pulse of $2 + 3$ goes like this:

Here are two examples of it:

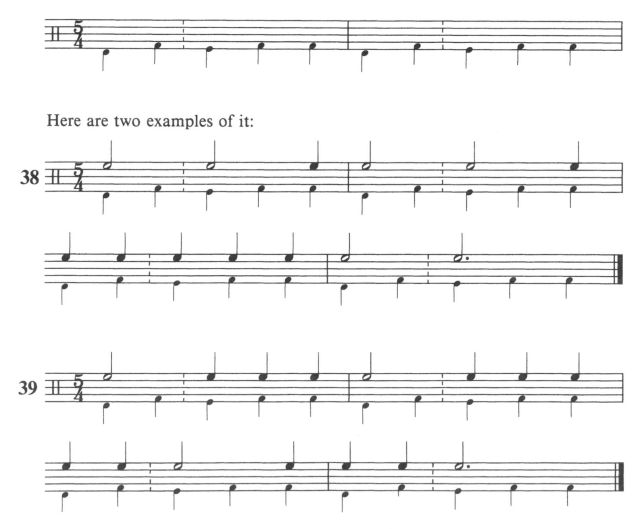

There is also a pulse of 3 + 2. It goes like this:

Here are two examples of it:

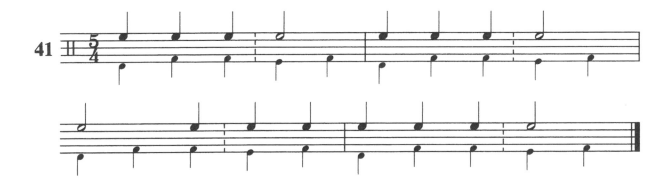

Make up one example of each. First 2 + 3:

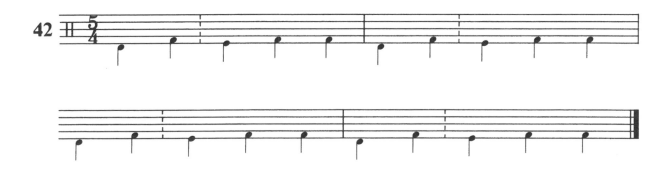

Next 3 + 2:

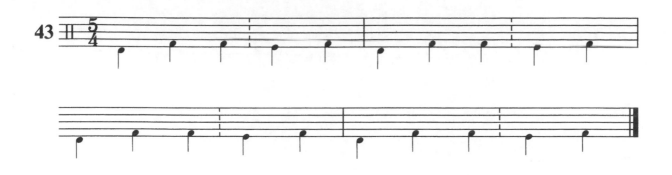

The two can also be mixed. Look at the broken bar line to tell whether it is 2 + 3 or 3 + 2:

or

What you have really done in the last two examples is mixing two-time with three-time. In the music of our time, meters change often. The number of beats is indicated at the beginning of each bar. If there is no new number it means that you continue the meter of the previous bar.

Let us try this with pulse alone first:

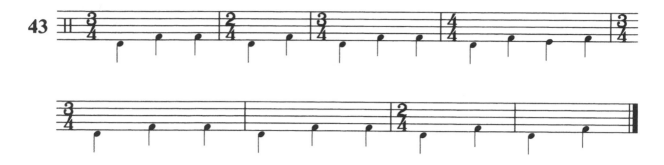

Now with an upper line:

and

Make up two examples of changing meters of your own. Write the pulse line first
— this is the first time you will be doing that — with the meter changes at the beginning of each bar. Then invent the upper line to go above the pulse.

All the book is giving you at this point are staff lines.

You do everything.

46

47

You have learned a great many different things about rhythm by now. You know how to keep a steady pulse, you have learned notes and rests of different length, you know about ties and different kinds of upbeats, and you are familiar with $\frac{2}{4}$, $\frac{3}{4}$, $\frac{4}{4}$, time as well as with different types of $\frac{5}{4}$ time and changing meters.

It is time to take a big step forward and to divide the beat into smaller notes.

B. DIVIDING THE BEAT INTO TWO EQUAL PARTS

VI. The Eighth-note in ²⁄₄ Time

When we divide the quarter beat into two equal parts, we get what

is called an eighth-note. It looks like this ♪♪

or like this: ♫

There can be more than two on one beam: ♫♫

Let us try some eighth-notes in ²⁄₄ time.

There is an eighth-rest.   It looks like this: ⅞

Eighth-notes can be tied across the bar line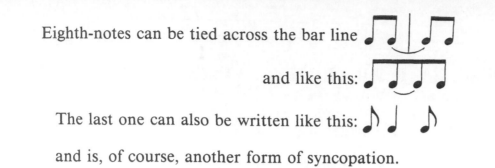

and like this:

The last one can also be written like this:

and is, of course, another form of syncopation.

Rests can also create the feeling of syncopation.

Just as a dot after a half-made it last for three quarter beats, a dot after a quarter-note will make it last for three eighth-notes. (For those who like mathematics it can be put as follows: the dot after a note adds half its value to it.) Here is an example with dotted quarter-notes:

A piece can begin with an eighth-note upbeat. When it does, it is a good idea to establish the pulse before beginning. Like this:

When a piece begins with a two-note upbeat in eighth-notes, the same should be done.

Also when it begins with a three-note upbeat in eighth-notes.

Here are a few examples with which to practice all these new skills:

Make up two examples of your own. Use eighth-notes, eighth rests, ties and syncopation.

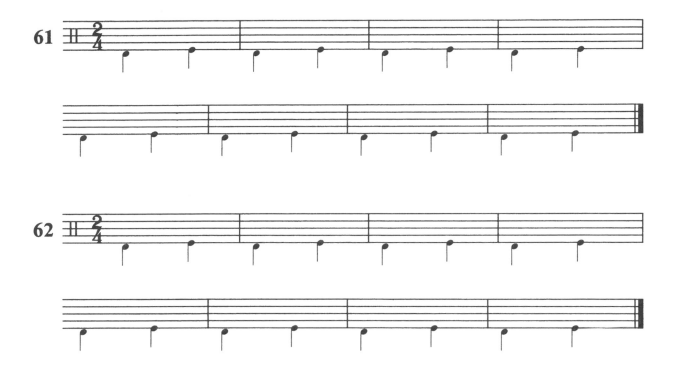

VII.   The Eighth-note in $\frac{3}{4}$ Time

In this chapter we shall practice eighth-notes in $\frac{3}{4}$ time.

30

Now with rests and ties:

and some syncopation:

A number of different upbeats are possible with the use of eighth-notes in triple time. Let us try just three of them.

In each case we want to establish the pulse securely before we begin; perhaps in silence, if we are alone.

A single note upbeat:

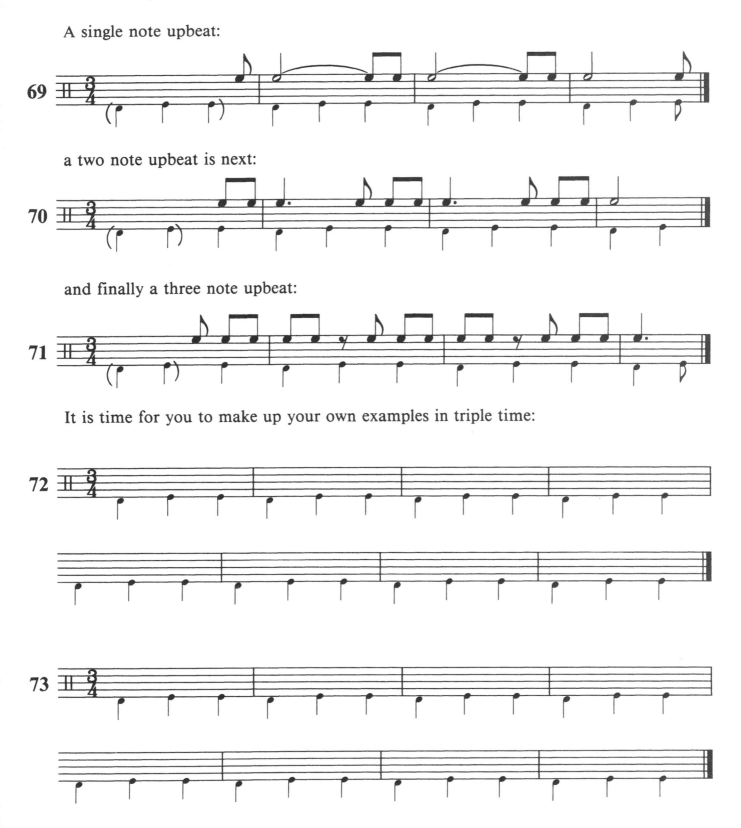

a two note upbeat is next:

and finally a three note upbeat:

It is time for you to make up your own examples in triple time:

32

VIII. The Eighth-note in 4/4 Time

There is really nothing new about eighth-notes in 4/4 time.

So here are several examples for practice. All of them have notes, rests, ties and a little syncopation here and there.

Here are a few short ones with upbeats:

And here is one for you to make up:

33

IX. The Eighth-note in $\frac{5}{4}$ Time and Changing Meters

To conclude the chapters with eighth-notes we must practice them in five-time and changing meters. Let us begin with five-time which is a combination of 2 and 3.

Now with five-time which is a combination of 3 and 2:

And now with changing meters:

Make up an example in which the meter changes every bar, or at least often, and which uses eighth-notes as well as quarter and half-notes. As you did in number 46, write the pulse line first with its meter changes and only after that is done, invent the upper line. The book is again providing you with nothing but blank staves.

88

C. DIVIDING THE BEAT INTO THREE EQUAL PARTS

X. The Triplet in $\frac{2}{4}$ Time and $\frac{6}{8}$ Meter, the "Hemiola"

The pulse can also be divided into three equal parts. When that happens, we call it a triplet. It looks like this

Two other patterns are possible   and

To practice the first of these you should know that it

is really the same as   performed on a single beat.

If you can do   accurately without beating the pulse,

you can perform

The same is true of the second pattern; it is the same as

performed on a single beat. Do it a few times without

beating the pulse and you will know it.   to

Let us practice triplets in $\frac{2}{4}$ meter:

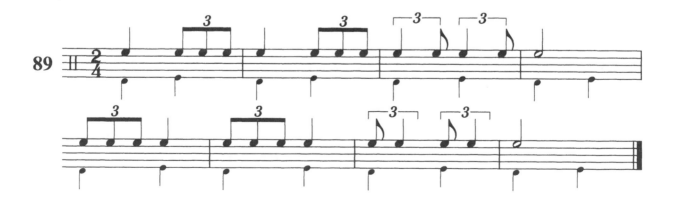

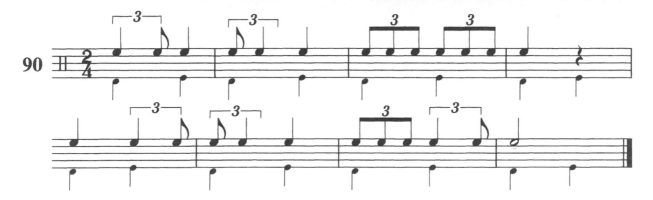

With the use of rests and ties many more rhythmic combinations become possible:

There can even be syncopation with triplets:

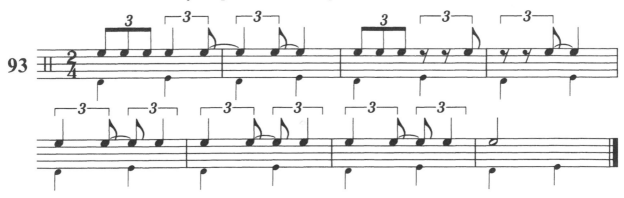

The last thing you just did is probably the most complex so far.

It is almost like two rhythms at the same time.

38

When a piece in $\frac{2}{4}$ time makes extensive use of triplets, it is often notated in $\frac{6}{8}$ time rather than in $\frac{2}{4}$. In that case the pulse is written in dotted quarter-notes. As you know, each of them is as long as three eighth-notes and the pulse looks like this:

Thus the following bars written in $\frac{2}{4}$ time

could also be written in $\frac{6}{8}$ time

A listener could not tell which of the two versions you were performing. They sound absolutely the same. The $\frac{6}{8}$ version looks simpler. $\frac{6}{8}$ meter has been popular at all times. Some people call it a compound meter because it has two beats but three notes on each of them.

Let us get familiar with $\frac{6}{8}$ time by practicing it. Of course there are rests and ties in it and we shall start using them right away.

Here is that rhythm again, the one you first encountered in No. 93, which is almost like two against three. It has been known since the time of Bach or before and is called a "Hemiola."

Time to make up your own examples. First, one in $\frac{2}{4}$ time which uses triplets.

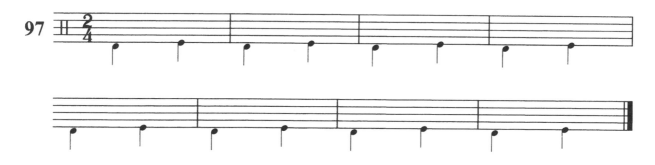

Now one in $\frac{6}{8}$ time. Try to use a "Hemiola"; it never happens in the last bar of anything. The bar just before the last is a likely spot to have one.

XI. The Triplet in $\frac{3}{4}$ Time and $\frac{9}{8}$ Meter

This chapter deals with triplets in $\frac{3}{4}$ time and its equivalent: $\frac{9}{8}$ time.

can also be written like this:

To the listener the two versions will sound absolutely identical. Notice that in the second bar of the $\frac{9}{8}$ version there was a tie although no barline was crossed. There is no other way to write a note that is to last for 9 beats, except to tie one that lasts for 6 to one that lasts for 3 beats.

Let us practice these without any further ado. We shall alternate examples in $\frac{3}{4}$ time with those in $\frac{9}{8}$ time.

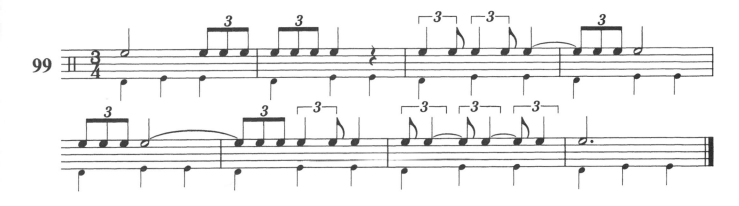

99

100

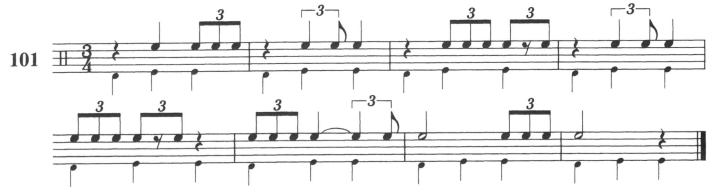

101

102

Time to make up your own; first one in $\frac{3}{4}$ time with triplets.

103

Then one in $\frac{9}{8}$ time

104

XII. The Triplet in $\frac{4}{4}$ Time and $\frac{12}{8}$ Meter; Changing Meters

In chapter XII we shall get acquainted with $\frac{12}{8}$ time which is, of course $\frac{4}{4}$ time with each beat (or some beats) divided into three. You probably don't need this, but here is one more example of two notations sounding exactly the same:

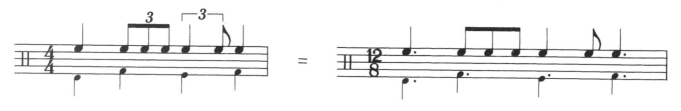

$\frac{12}{8}$ meter has been very popular since the time of Bach.

Let us have just one example in $\frac{4}{4}$ time; all the others in $\frac{12}{8}$.

A rest lasting for three eighth-notes can look like this: ⁊

It can also be a quarter-note rest with a dot: ⁊·

So far we have used only the first; now we shall use both.

A whole note with a dot lasts for six quarter beats or twelve eighth-notes. There is one in the next example.

44

108

And now space for your own example:

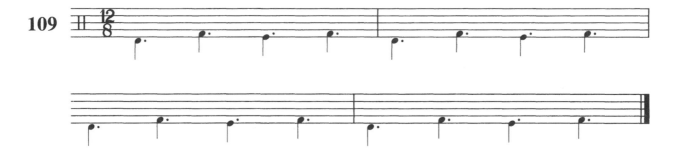

109

Twelve is the largest number you will find in this book as part of meter indications. There is such a thing as $\frac{15}{8}$ time and $\frac{18}{8}$ time but we shall not worry about them at the moment. What we do need to practice is changing meters with $\frac{6}{8}$, $\frac{9}{8}$ and $\frac{12}{8}$ time.

110

111

D. DIVIDING THE BEAT INTO FOUR EQUAL PARTS

XIII. The Sixteenth-note in $\frac{2}{4}$ Time; More Syncopation

When we divide the pulse into four equal parts, we get sixteenth-notes. They look

like this: ♪♪♪♪ or like that: ♫♫

There are three basic patterns:

They are really quicker versions of familiar rhythms. To get them right it might be helpful to go through the three stages indicated below:

Stage 1: **Stage 2:** **Stage 3:**

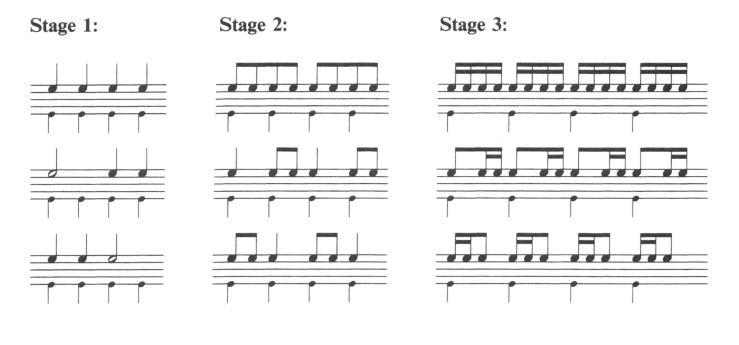

Let us try them in $\frac{2}{4}$ time

With use of a dotted eighth-note (as long as 3 sixteenth-notes) and a touch of syncopation three more patterns become available:

To comprehend them fully let us take them through the same three stages

Stage 1:   **Stage 2:**   **Stage 3:**

Let us practice patterns 4, 5 and 6:

There is a sixteenth-rest. This is how it looks:

We have had dotted quarter-notes and dotted eighth-notes. Now we shall meet a double-dotted quarter-note which is as long as seven sixteenths:

(The first dot added half the value of the quarter-note to it: an eighth. The second dot added half the value of that, namely a sixteenth.)

To perform the following double-dotted rhythm accurately, it is helpful to subdivide the pulse:

With a good musician you can always tell the difference among the following three rhythms:

A number of different upbeats using sixteenth-notes are possible. Here are the three most common ones. Do establish the pulse firmly in each case:

Sixteenth-notes can be tied within the bar and across the bar line and with the use of rests and ties we get an almost unlimited number of rhythmic possibilities.

Not so easy? Well, it shows you how much you have learned. There are many more examples with sixteenth-notes to come. First make up two of your own in $\frac{2}{4}$ time.

XIV.   The Sixteenth-note in $\frac{3}{4}$ Time

The last chapter was long and introduced a great many new things, not all of them easy. It might be a good idea to go over them again in the same order, only now in $\frac{3}{4}$ time.

Let us do just that.

Here are the first three, the simple patterns:

Now the three more complex patterns:

Now rests, ties and a touch of syncopation:

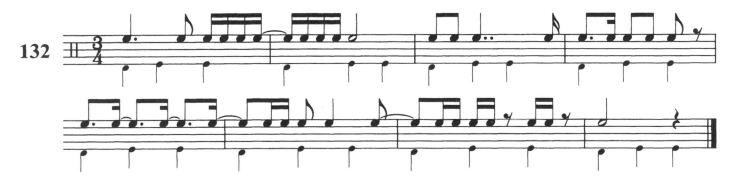

52

Several different upbeats:

Now two for you to make up

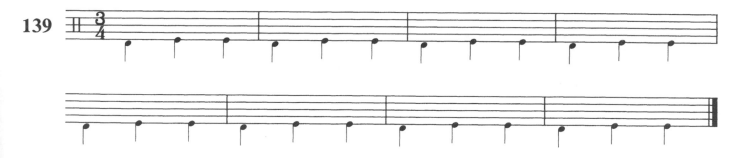

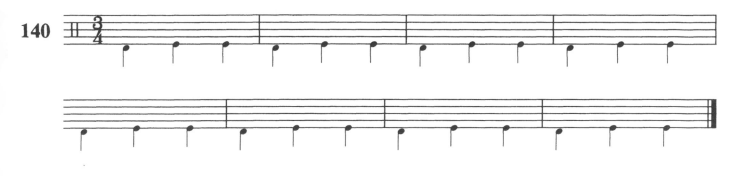

XV. The Sixteenth-note in $\frac{4}{4}$ Time

In this chapter we shall practice sixteenth-note rhythms and rests in $\frac{4}{4}$ time.

And now one for you to make up:

XVI. The Sixteenth-note with Changing Meters

In this, our last chapter, we want to practice everything you have learned with changing meters.

149

Here are some blank staff lines for the last example you will make up in this book. Use notes, rests, ties, syncopation and do not forget to change the meter.

150

If you want to develop your rhythmic ability further, you are now ready for chapter V in my other book, RHYTHMIC TRAINING. It will teach you to mix divisions of the beat (triplets with eighth- or sixteenth-notes), to divide the beat into five, six, seven and more equal parts; it will teach you how to change the rate of the pulse and, eventually, how to perform two rhythms at the same time.